Violin

ORANGE BLOSSOM SPECIAL
(A Hillbilly Concert Piece)
For Violin and Piano

Words and Music by ERVIN T. ROUSE
Arranged by EUGENE JELESNIK

Violin

ORANGE BLOSSOM SPECIAL
(A Hillbilly Concert Piece)
For Violin and Piano *

Words and Music by ERVIN T. ROUSE
Arranged by EUGENE JELESNIK

Fast, in real hillbilly style!

* Special Accompaniment for 3 Clarinets, Piano, Guitar, Bass and Drums available on Rental.

ORANGE BLOSSOM SPECIAL

A Hillbilly Concert Piece for Violin and Piano

Words and Music by
ERVIN T. ROUSE

Arranged by Eugene Jelesnik

UNIVERSAL

**UNIVERSAL MUSIC
PUBLISHING GROUP**
www.universalmusicpublishing.com

EXCLUSIVELY DISTRIBUTED BY